Martha in the Mirror

ALSO BY RENEE NORMAN

Backhand Through the Mother (2007)
True Confessions (2005)
*House of Mirrors: Performing Autobiograph(icall)y in
   Language/Education* (2001)

Martha in the Mirror

poems by

Renee Norman

inanna poetry & fiction series
INANNA Publications and Education Inc.
Toronto, Canada

Copyright © 2010 Renee Norman

Except for the use of short passages for review purposes, no part of this book may be reproduced, in part or in whole, or transmitted in any form or by any means, electronically or mechanically, including photocopying, recording, or any information or storage retrieval system, without prior permission in writing from the publisher.

 Canada Council for the Arts / Conseil des Arts du Canada

 ONTARIO ARTS COUNCIL / CONSEIL DES ARTS DE L'ONTARIO

The publisher gratefully acknowledges the support of the Canada Council for the Arts and the Ontario Arts Council for its publishing program.

The publisher is also grateful for the kind support received from an Anonymous Fund at The Calgary Foundation.

Library and Archives Canada Cataloguing in Publication

Norman, Renee
    Martha in the mirror : poems / by Renee Norman.

(Inanna poetry and fiction series)
ISBN 978-1-926708-11-9

    1. Quest, Martha (Fictitious character)--Poetry. 2. Lessing, Doris, 1919- --Poetry.
I. Title. II. Series: Inanna poetry and fiction series

PS8627.O77M37 2010   C811'.6   C2010-901274-7

Cover design by Valerie Fullard

Printed and bound in Canada

Inanna Publications and Education Inc.
210 Founders College, York University
4700 Keele Street
Toronto, Ontario, Canada M3J 1P3
Telephone: (416) 736-5356 Fax (416) 736-5765
Email: inanna@yorku.ca Website: www.yorku.ca/inanna

For Don
(Still counting the years)

Contents

Prelude: Exorcising Martha	3
Martha, in White	7
I Am the Land	8
Between Friends	9
Between Wor(l)ds	11
Mother	12
Martha, Leaving	14
Martha's Father	16
The Mouse Ran Up the Clock	18
Assignation	20
Dream Moments	21
Dear Doris Lessing 1	22
Martha Answers	23
These Women in the Mirror	24
By Way of Explanation	26
Till Death Do Us Part	27
Messages from Martha	29
Postscript from Martha	31

Lost	32
On the Edge	33
Through the Crib Bars	35
Dear Doris Lessing 2	38
Martha in England	39
Lost Landscapes	40
Invocation	41
In the House on Radlett Street	42
Confetti	45
Caroline's Dream	47
Dear Doris Lessing 3	49
Martha's Journal I	50
Between the Lines	52
Martha's Journal II	53
Emotional Reconstruction	54
On the Rug of Madness	56
Autobiography and Psychiatry	57
Martha in the Mirror	59
For Martha's Ears Only	60
Echoes	61
What I Dream for Her	62
Acknowledgements	65

*Poems written upon inhabiting Martha Quest,
the protagonist of Doris Lessing's Martha Quest novels,
the* Children of Violence *series.*

Prelude: Exorcising Martha

I spent the summer with Martha Quest. I grew up with her in the wild veld of Southern Rhodesia as she fought her mother, witnessed her wedding out of haste and habit, celebrated at the birth of her daughter, mourned when she abandoned her along with a loveless marriage. I sympathized when her father, a war veteran, succumbed to further illness, still embraced her as she embraced communism, a second loveless marriage, an errant lover. I understood her disillusionment following the war, as she prepared to move to England.

In the first volume of her autobiography, Doris Lessing states that all one needs to do to know her life is to read the Martha Quest books. She explains that a particular person is so and so in this story, in that book. She describes the straw yellow of someone's hair, the scene in a hospital. Read it in the books.

No, she will not tell you the real name of a character in one of those books, as she writes about the part this character played in her own life, because the person is now ensconced in high society. Yes, this person whom she admires so greatly is the same Greek character in her Martha books, and in tribute to him, she acknowledges the connection. As I read the autobiography, I began to recognize bits from the novels before Lessing placed them for the reader. I know who this is, or, I see now how Martha's mother came to be written as she was. Or, yes, I felt

Lessing's grief over the two of her three children whom she left when I read that Martha left her fictional child. Each Martha Quest book became a kind of "golden notebook" of her life for me, a narrative collage overlapped with the autobiography. As a reader I lost myself in that autobiography as if I were steeped in my summer reading of the Martha books, and it was a powerful experience.

I discovered Doris Lessing late, just as I came late to the writing that is now a central part of my life. It was worth the wait, because I brought a lifetime of my own experience to Martha and Doris' lives. Intertwined among the three of them is all that has happened to us over the years.

As I wrote about Martha, this character I lifted and borrowed from Doris Lessing, it was still me who snuck into the poems, creeping in unannounced not only between the lines and stanzas, but offering details and impressions and emotions of my own life for Martha to use, a curiously freeing and uncensored experience. Writing the Martha poems meant I could leave big gaps and open spaces for Martha and me to move around in.

And so I encountered Martha in the mirror. This mirror reflected back the Martha of Lessing's Bildungsromane, as I read and interpreted her; the Martha who is in me; and my selves as they filter through Martha's reflection. These Marthas come to light in the mirror of writing, a process at times metaphoric, at times metonymic.

And so I entered Martha, inhabiting her like a spirit for a series of poems. These poems are as much about me as about Martha, or Doris, and I found that in the process of exorcising Martha from the books and giving her a newly re-written life in my poems, I was also exorcising even more of me. I was also considering all I have never been. There are so many differences between Martha and me. And yet, and yet.... Within the differences, there are mirrors that reflect back metonymic parts of the body of humanity and living, frames of resemblance whose wavering silvery pictures are both one thing and another at once, a doubling. This doubling is both a presence and an absence, both inside and outside the frames.

Martha is a mirror. And in the mirror, Martha is double. Martha is also the Other. This is the other of *écriture feminine*. This is the Other of the female body, which in Hélène's Cixous' terms, is written and is already text. I invite you to enter the mirror of this writing, Martha and I in mirrors.

Martha, in White

she has sewn a white gown for herself
the vestal virgin of discontent
she dances in this bridal skin
out of a mudhut home

floats over the deeper mud in the rains
still unsullied
except for spatters on the hem

like blood they stain the white fabric
weigh down the gauze of the dress
with fingertips heavy and black
as if someone is dragging her back, back
snipping the threads she worked so carefully
exposing all her darkness
underneath

I Am the Land

this mud, the rains
the heat of the veld
and the movement of a jacaranda tree
throb in her heart
the rhythm through centuries of weather-beaten abuse
on skin
the country the scarred back of a monkey-kaffir —
skin like muck
trod upon —
sucks her in
covers her head
she breathes moist earth
loose from the plough of footsteps running
hers

Between Friends

he lends Martha books
the latest in socialist trends
between navy blue hard covers
that replace the childhood games of their youth
books held against her chest
to block his gaze at her new breasts

does he daily chant the Jewish prayer
which thanks God
for not being born a woman
as he lectures her on dialectical materialism
and the plight of the worker?

it is his smouldering Jewishness
as much as the books
which attract her over and over
to his father's store
the old man (eyebrows raised)
peering at her from beneath his yarmulke
distrustful of another Gentile shiksah
in a land where white supremacy
is draped like carpet across the veld

with Marx and Engels and
the trouble in Spain they spar

his passion to bend her thoughts
turn another kind of prayer

Between Wor(l)ds

in book time
between wor(l)ds
books stacked like steps
around the architecture of her rented room
Martha does not sleep
snacks on sentences
all night long

gone is the flat line drawing of her day
the structure of the office
the symmetry of a prim supervisor
the tailored suits
on cool skin

in her nylon slip
she climbs and climbs the words
a stairway to her reformation
amazed at first light of morning
to be identical
she has not moved at all

Mother

the word lays claim to Martha
a heavy breastplate of armour
encircling her
until she finds it hard to breathe
sometimes she wants to slap her mother
throw the nearest object
at those two nervous chattering
lines of lip
which always seem to dribble criticism:
        the unsuitable close fit of your dress, Martha
        the wildness that sends you to those books,
        those ideas, Martha
        can't you just settle down with the child
        and welcome matronhood

Motherhood

the word like a drawstring pulled tight
and then unfastened
back and forth between
the chafe of strangulation
and the freedom of relief
        love with anger
           edginess with pride
           ownership with fear

Martha pulls away
from the endless tugging
her mother's thin body
birdlike over a hundred broken dreams

laying the sharp sudden burn
of a noose
letting go

Martha, Leaving

mama

she can hear the bleat
like a lamb
knows the thumb will find its way
to the bottomless hollow of mouth
sees the diapers hanging to dry
unfolded, white
flags of surrender

she can feel the small body weight
pressed against the ache of her breasts
though her hands are empty

but flung out
weightless
no longer attached to the part of her
that thinks
limbs
drooping out of embroidered nightgowns

she remembers the calendar on the wall
months of softness
of pink and blue wool
knitted into patterns
the smell of fresh, innocent powder
through the sharp yellow of urine
that spot on the neck

where she buried her nose
to breathe baby

she feels and remembers all of it
as she watches her hands
break through the door
to air

Martha's Father

the boy-man damaged by war
& the Englishman who emigrated
to Southern Rhodesia
with a Queen Anne chair

he is a heat sensor
who reflects Martha's change in temperature
or a veil that is drawn
to distance confrontation

he knows the restlessness in her
but did not question her marriage
did not pass judgement either
when she left the child

deep in a drug-induced sleep
he mutters wisdom
awake he offers nightmares

fingers that accuse
stakes of the fallen walls
around his body
his mind's grasp

of the horror he brings home to her

when she reads the first documented accounts
of Hitler's atrocities
it is her father's ribcage she envisions
every bone of Adam
another finger pointing

The Mouse Ran Up the Clock

Martha knows how to wait
in doctor's offices
men's beds
over bitter cups of coffee in cafés
by all the sidestreets and alleyways
leading to a different world
the waiting is a virus
in her blood
that spreads

like many women
she lives behind the clock hands where they meet
as if that overlap
were protection from a lapse

once a woman said:
*you're frightening the mothers picking up their children
at the church —
are you meeting someone here?
can't you wait somewhere else?*

she moved away
an excommunicated mouse
felt her cheeks burn with shame

knew for a moment what it meant
to be black

how the waiting must have flushed through her
eyes red with desperation
the mothers thought she'd steal their precious children

like the dog in Cadiz, Spain
who at last count had waited 7 years
outside the hospital where his master died
Martha knows how to wait

Assignation

he enters Martha
as he might a room
where the light is blinding his eyes

in the tub he draws circles on her skin
with the soap
laughing he tells her
on his way to meet her
approached and propositioned
"I said I already have a lady"

he pushes small beds together
holds Martha where the space between them
forms a crevice
a hard ridge of earth
she feels beneath her back
overpowering his tender hold

in this scented
sinkhole talking
the pronoun I rings in her ears

it is then she knows the future
her skin round with dried white foam

Dream Moments

Martha felt his absence keenly
when next day
the meeting over
he looked at her
stubborn, unhappy
defiant
a kind of unperceptive dullness
in his eyes
missed moments
that's what she feared most
from these encounters

in her dream his kiss
so fierce
grabbed the unresolved feeling
between them
crushed it in the physical act of embrace

today
her arms empty
like a baby torn from a loving grip
he stood there
only a dream away

Dear Doris Lessing 1

Doris —
I am borrowing Martha
am writing autobiographical episodes
under her name
an alias for my own indiscretions

Doris —
I am signing her out
like a library book
opening her chapters
bending the corners of pages
and reading them backwards

Doris —
I am borrowing Martha
will not return her in the same condition
although she's long overdue

Martha Answers

you think you know me so well
as you sit in your house
with your middle class life

that wasn't me
why are you tainting me
with your own pathetic stories
waiting in the churchyard
and hauling out my parents, my friends
for re-inspection
changing Doris' history

what do you know of war
or injustice
I grew up with spilled blood in my veins
& crushed skulls for breakfast

rug fluff in an ovary
you were not even born
how dare you invade my soul

These Women in the Mirror

while Hannah* was interned
in a Parisian detainment camp
dreaming of a lost lover
who signed Nazi memos
Martha/Doris distributed pamphlets
in the Black district
wondering if her children
placed their baby teeth
under pillows not-too-late at night

and Dorothy** wrote poems and practised politics
only feeling free
the moment she learned of her husband's demise

I was not yet born
into this women's world
an egg latent in my mother's womb
rocked in forgotten memory
on an immigrant ship

how is it
without ears yet formed
I heard these women calling
from a choric past

years before I met them
on the mirror of a page

*German Jewish political theorist Hannah Arendt
**Canadian poet Dorothy Livesay

By Way of Explanation

oh, Martha
it's true
I did not flee
or starve
or smell the gas
nor bear witness
to horrors in the night
the everydayness of evil

but I was born from it
my grandparents' legacy
this darkness
belongs to all of us

Till Death Do Us Part

she wakes to his snores
air sucked into a rhinoceros
her elbow in his back
a pencil pointed
writing her dislike

no, it is not dislike, distaste
strong and bitter
with baked edges

the baby cries out
in her sleep, briefly
a clarion
that returns her to the domestic
no, she has undone
the apron of dumb acceptance

she can smell the beer
the smoke
on the long drawn-out breath
of another gigantic
hippopotamus

repelled
by the injustice in his freedom

to make such a zzzz
she creeps around in her mind
gathering twigs of hatred
to fuel her blaze

Messages from Martha

Martha wants to tell me
how her body was stolen
when she got pregnant
how she could not find
the bone on the inside of her ankle
for months the pressure
of her finger searching
left a dent
like poking around in the stuffing
of a cooked turkey

Martha wants me to know
it was not her choice
that women should throw up
blow up
stretch beyond all that could be imagined
until the skin on her belly
pulled parchment-thin
was a hot air balloon
about to explode in letters

and Martha wants me to know
every night when I arrange the blankets
round the fireplace of a small reddened cheek
and run my hand along the stove

of a dear damp forehead
I am touching the body
the bone
the heat of her scripture

Postscript from Martha

you re-write me with those words
that pen
I cannot see
I will draw it
with my words
that pen
red   waterproof
uni-ball fineliner
a fine line that
writing fine lines
with a fineliner
that pen
these words:

MY PAIN IS NOT FOR GENERAL CONSUMPTION
WHAT I WANT YOU TO KNOW YOU CANNOT FATHOM

Lost

I am so deep
in this place
I wonder if
I'll find my way out
is this a kind of madness?

one distorted funhouse mirror
after another
it's hard not to write maudlin
pitiful   snivelly

but that's my Picasso face
that stares back
at my pen
one eye on top
the nose and a forehead
split in half
by the time it's taken
to find my way back

On the Edge

the top of the car is folded down
like a quilt on a close night
the summer sun
follows her home
in the rearview mirror
too bright in her eyes
despite dark glasses

a shining pinpoint of light
it does not fade
along the roadway
its flashing light atop her vehicle
signals alarm

with reverse glances
she checks
what does this signify:
a moon on a black-shadowed night
a candle lit on a cake
in a darkened room
a beacon in a window
that beckons her home
this way the light summons
through an open curtain
this way, home

when she turns up the driveway
she has set the sun aside
for another warmth

much later
she remembers how
the mirror caught the glare in her eyes

Through the Crib Bars

I.
her pink cheeks
leak through the crib bars
asleep at last
as if she hadn't been screaming
that colicky high-pitched wail
only moments ago

shadows of the rails
fall down across her small back
with weightless rods
that imprison her to Martha's care
for an instant
Martha sees the stripes
as lashes from a whip
she shakes the image off
with loathing

afraid to touch the soft skin
for fear she'll wake
and start the cycle again
too soon
she dreams the baby is pliant
molded to her ribs
like putty
more like the babies in the books

with four-hour schedules
and gurgles
not this fierce creature
hard to hold
impossible to cuddle

II.
she calls the baby's name
through the leafy openings in the hedge
a kind of lament
whispered in the floral underworld
but the baby doesn't respond
already she has forgotten Martha
forgotten the vessel

her curls are looser now
the head upright
she sits unaided
fist tight around a plastic toy
slick from saliva
Martha misses her
more than she would have thought possible
a pink baby from some magazine
Martha feels pain that someone
accomplished what she didn't

III.
the rules are that she must observe
from a distance
(her mother makes that clear)
when Martha sees the child
placed on her father's sickbed daily
a small body curved into
her father's emaciated thigh
she can smell the camphor of the medicines
hovering
and her mother's servitude

IV.
in the photos a stranger with Martha's eyes
glances back
good-byes made
years ago

Dear Doris Lessing 2

Doris —
years ago a woman told me her story she walked out one day
away from a loveless marriage and two young children just
a toothbrush in her purse a man we worked with knew this
story too one day wandered into my office dazed and slightly
drunk sputtering how could she how could she I thought I
detected regret in his eyes and possibility too
do you?

Martha in England

she is not the Martha I met
on the pages of Southern Rhodesian veld
this second Martha walks
into the novel of an English family's life
hidden in the complications
of their British citizens' lives

it is not the Martha
I have welded into being
all regret and pain and memory
as if with this new landscape
one which her mother and father
breathed into her infant lungs
she can exhale with ease
the heat, sweat, wounds, iron
of Jacob's Burg

Lost Landscapes

Martha!
I call her name
in the séance of this poem
invoking the spirit
of her land
the heat of Southern Rhodesian sun
beyond the damp grey English rains

my own memory of landscape
is patched
onto my first flight away from the parched prairie
the pull of the plane
into the altitude of the unknown
swelled with sorrow

neither of us could bear to leave
or stay
knowing that if we grew
into the moist soil of wet places
our selves and souls would keep
from burning dry

Invocation

I am the ghost you seek
the face you see in the mirror
doubled
a spirit
      a soul
a sprite
      a blight
not text
      a word
a letter
      a sound

a cry

In the House on Radlett Street

I cannot stay long
Martha's caution to the household
a distance she required
unencumbered
was the word she conjured

the word transformed:
entrenched
in long years
where she seldom remembered the initial warning

the Martha
who had walked the streets of London
for days hungry
exhausted
inside herself reaching
deep into a core of fresh apple flesh

though this middle-aged Martha
had nothing to show
for years of service
just prune-dried skin on her hands
she was an apple doll on a stick
stuck away inside
someone's bottom drawer

in the house on Radlett Street

but not ill-treated
not at all
likely would be missed
if she left
a part of dinner parties
and family plans
daughter of Eve
she had grown from seedling
to oak
whose leaves
changing colour
signalled each new season in the house
blending in to the stable colors

but Martha knew
it was a doll's existence
the way she played house
as a child
mother of dolls
wife of playmates
and nothing real to call her own
at the end of the day
when carriage was wheeled

back into the corner
lifeless because the players
had disappeared
to families of their own

Confetti

more important
than the people she sees through gauze
in her interior life
she visits corridors of memory
that twist and turn
a maze of pain
re-visited again and again
every phrase
facial movement
a remembered piece to complete the puzzle

aloud she names no part of flesh
so when her daughter's name
appears on a peace march placard
CAROLINE
she reads it like a newspaper
eager for the first glimpse of the day
but easily placed upon the fireplace hearth

later when she revolves
in the tunnel of madness her introspection has arranged
that sign will appear
from the top of a ten foot window
distraught
she plunges to the grassy dreams
of half-asleep, half-awake

and alive, broken
she eats the excrement of ashes blowing
high letters tiny print
CAROLINE caroline
burnt confetti of a lost child

Caroline's Dream

vaguely Caroline recalled
the shelter of a small flat
enveloped in the white detergent
and mist of drying diapers
a hand
sometimes gentle
arranged folds around her shoulders
feet
it felt more dream than memory
inhabiting that blank, empty space
in her grandmother's eyes

sometimes her grandmother stared
through Caroline hard
hatred palpable
for seconds standing there between them
like a wall
then dissolved in the returned good humour
of a capable
grandparent

she knew the gentle hand of the dream
not her grandmother's
not her father's or stepmother's
that held pink and blue wool
nursery rhymes sweet milk and honey

if only she could remember more
openly ask
without causing the closed looks
her questions aroused
the pained faces to the wall

if only she could reach
for that hand
and pull it down
to eye the face connected
to the touch

Dear Doris Lessing 3

Doris —
how does one explain a toothbrush?
to brush away the anguish
in a tongue?
teeth bared

Martha's Journal I

full of people
Caroline does not know
rambling rows of letters
a diatribe of impressions
feelings political
statements

words scratched out
like she was

Caroline hunts
for her own name
some reference
to the pain of separation
but finds only
what is not recorded here

a mother tongue tastes
whatever is brought to it
one day it laps up
the milk of kindness
(how Martha must have suffered)
another (bad) morning
it licks the blood
of childish wounds
a vampire organ

it feeds on the tender
(how hard a woman Martha
must have been)
the attempt at truth
swallowed up by silence

Between the Lines

my silence
speaks
listen
you will hear
what is not recorded
what you cannot
understand
can you forgive?

Martha's Journal II

one page holds some notes:
a baby's sleep patterns
up so early every morning
its constant needs
relentless
the hardship

this slaps Caroline
a branch held back
then given full release
she lurches forward
a child who always rose
as late as possible
who never complained
about playing alone
a perfect child for any mother

she rips out the page
a weed in the imaginary garden
of some children's story

Emotional Reconstruction

in China mothers hold
broken glass frames
of their children
to their pierced hearts
the glass missing
from those frames
part of the rubble
in Sichuan
sharp pieces, debris
the sad humus
of an unrepentant matriarchal earth

She takes what She will
with such unspoken speed
no warning
to precede what will be
the last walk to school
the final wave and kiss

recovered Hello Kitty knapsacks
stand in a row
backs, arms buried
in the destruction
this graveyard of canvas
absence

what is our pain
in the wake of such absolute destruction
powerful loss

On the Rug of Madness

one reddened leaf
suspended in the air
on the finger of a spider web
this is what Martha thinks
lying on the rug
in the midst of their madness
this is the place
where Lynda always lives
Martha visits
the dying green
the plunge off the great grasping
hands of a tree
caught on the happenstance
of this limb of web
not clinging precarious
desperate or afraid
but waiting
for the sensation
of the rest of the fall

Autobiography and Psychiatry

he needs the rest of her autobiography
for his report
(that's what he tells her)
30 minutes
she deliberately leaves out
events   details   trauma
that raw place
can't take even a finger

she is struck
he calls this history-taking
autobiography
moved even
he does not know
her work
she senses the psychic
in psychiatry
wants to ask him
questions

instead she reconstructs
her life
a truth here
omission there

she knows with certainty

autobiography
like psychiatry
is an inexact endeavour
depends on how
we present our/selves
what we are willing
to open

and the rest
the hidden
the terrible secrets
deep silences
an autobiography
of the not-yet-said

Martha in the Mirror

Martha in the mirror
is a young girl
expected to do so well at school
a young woman drinking dancing
at sundowners carefree alive
a young wife and mother
with a sense of purpose

Then, who drew these lines on a neck?
this pouch that sags
underneath a chin?
weatherbeaten hands that must belong
to some farm labourer
and a thin frame no longer voluptuous
just thin

image is reflected back
again and again
in the disinterested glances of men
who quickly look away
children whose faces never light up
at airport terminals

this 3-way mirror
exposes every sharp angle of relationship

For Martha's Ears Only

if she were to take shape
in my room
I would whisper
the only two words that fit

I am not Martha
not a child of war
seeking solace
not Martha
trapped in a loveless marriage
or oppressed by children's petulance

yet if she rose off the pages
swelling in novel possibilities
I would recognize
the limbs hers
a composite heart transplanted
where a person is most worthy
of the color of her skin
the cold ungentle parts of her
that worded me
and whisper:
I understand

Echoes

a word

    a letter

        a sound

            a cry

What I Dream for Her

it's not what I dreamed for her
this grey doomed climate
following Martha
over the mud of the veld
youthful rebellion dried by marriage and motherhood
the releasing rains of communism and lovers
in a spectacular rainbow of abandonment
finally to become
housekeeper-cum-lover-cum-friend
a dull autumn in a brilliant succession
of seasons

there have to be some other endings
not failed marriages
not dead lovers
not lost children
this whirlwind of the past
a cyclone of madness

I want to give her
mild temperatures
the contentment of a daughter's warm back
lodged up against her own

solid earth
under the fallen leaves
of a home of her own
and love,
a cloudburst of love

Acknowledgements

Some of these poems and parts of the prelude have appeared in their current or altered form in the following book and journals:

House of Mirrors (Peter Lang Publ.)
Language and Literacy Journal (Queen's University)
Whetstone Journal

The following three poems received first place in Whetstone's Literary Contest:

"Martha, in White"
"Mother"
"Martha, Leaving"

With thanks: to my family, especially three wonderful and ever-supportive young women, daughters Sara, Rebecca, and Erin, and a husband with uncommon generosity, Don. To poets and mentors extraordinaire, George McWhirter and Carl Leggo. And to fabulous and visionary editor, Luciana Ricciutelli.

Photo: Sara Norman

Renee Norman, Ph.D., is an award-winning poet, a writer, and a teacher. Her first volume of poetry, *True Confessions*, was awarded the prestigious Helen and Stan Vine Canadian Jewish Book Award for Poetry in 2006. In 2007, her second volume of poetry, *Backhand Through the Mother*, was published. Her doctoral dissertation, *House of Mirrors: Performing Autobiograph(icall)y in Language/Education*, received the Canadian Association for Curriculum Studies Distinguished Dissertation Award and was published in 2001. Renee's poetry, stories, and articles have been published widely in literary and academic journals, anthologies and newspapers. Currently, Renee is a literacy consultant for Vancouver School Board. She lives in Coquitlam, British Columbia, with her daughters and husband.